AF505307

The Power
Of
Your Words

Published by Brolga Publishing Pty Ltd
ABN 46 063 962 443
PO Box 12544
A'Beckett St
Melbourne, VIC, 8006
Australia

email: markzocchi@brolgapublishing.com.au

National Library of Australia Cataloguing-in-Publication entry

Author: Affirmation Angel
Title: The power of your words : light hearted inspiration from an Angel's point of view / Affirmation Angel.
ISBN: 9781922175410 (hardback)
Subjects: Inspiration.
          Self-consciousness (Awareness)
          Kindness.
          Conduct of life.
Dewey Number: 153.4

Printed in China
Cover design by Chameleon Print Design

BE PUBLISHED

Publish through a successful publisher. National distribution, Macmillan & International distribution to the United Kingdom, North America. Sales Representation to South East Asia
Email: markzocchi@brolgapublishing.com.au

The Power
Of
Your Words

❧

Affirmation Angel

A fun, quirky, imaginary Angel

Lighthearted inspiration

...from an Angel's point of view

Contents Page

A Word from the Angel

I am an Affirmation Angel, there are quite a few of us around. We listen to affirmations and make them happen. However, you don't always say what you want.

You think you do, but when we present you with what you have asked for, you say it's all wrong and we get disappointed.

In our realm we have no concept of time, so when asking for something, you need to be specific.

People ask for 'rich'. We have heard you say a cake is rich, is that what you mean?

We are discovering that wealth means different things for many different people. Wealth to a homeless person is different to wealth to a stockbroker.

Be exact with what you want.
We get a lot of requests for 'slim'. Again this means different things to different people.

Quite frankly, we don't understand fat and slim, pretty or ugly.

You are perfect to us.

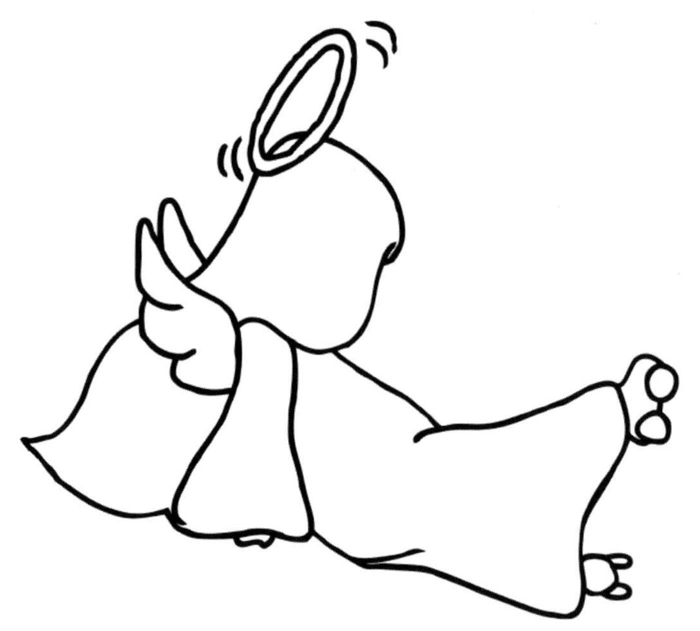

Try not to say, "I never have an accident," as an apprentice may just hear 'accident' and think you want one.

Better to say, "I drive safely."

The same applies to remembering things.
Instead of, "I mustn't forget" say, "I will remember."

To be on time, ask us to help you be punctual, not just telling us you don't want to be late.

Leave no confusion for you or the Angel.

I have to go now, so much to do.

www.affirmationangel.com

The Power of Words

The words we use affect us physically, mentally and emotionally. We are primed from childhood to respond in certain ways to things that are said. What we say then becomes what we believe.

You can't do that!
That's ridiculous.
You'll never do that.
You'll always be broke.
You will never amount to anything.
Don't forget.

That great 'don't' word.

Let me ask you to do something. Sit down and think about this. Don't think of a red dress, don't think of a red Ferrari, you know the one with a black horse on it.

Most people will think of the red dress or the Ferrari. This is not psychobabble; this is simply the way the brain works. You cannot tell the brain 'don't' as it will picture it anyway. If you say, "Don't forget your keys," the brain will picture you forgetting your keys. If you say, "Don't have an accident'" the brain will picture an accident. The process works better if you say to yourself, " I remember my keys." "I drive safely."

If you want your child to remember things, for example you want your child to bring home a book, ask the child to remember the book and then go through the steps.

Remember to pick a book,
Remember to put the book in your bag.
Remember to bring it home.

Encourage them to picture themselves picking up the book and putting it in the bag and then bringing it home. Remembering is important, not the forgetting. I drive safely; the brain will see you safely driving yourself. Concentrate on the safety not the accident.

The brain is an incredible part of the body, we are still learning about its capabilities. Many books are written on the amazing studies of the brain. One study is in a book called 'The Winners Bible,' written by a doctor. He explains that there are goggles that can be worn that turn the view of the wearer upside down. Within three days of wearing them, the brain can work out how to turn everything the right way up. You don't have to do anything to make this happen. You don't have to tell the brain to fix it. It just does. If the brain can do that, what else is it capable of?

It's hard to believe things can change, when you're not getting anywhere, and you feel that something has zapped all the life out of you. Start to observe people around you who use affirmations see how they work for them.

Make statements, write them down, and say them daily.

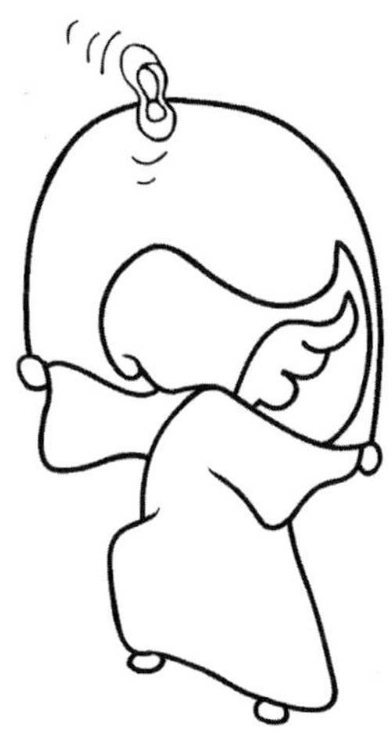

Good Things Happen, If You Believe They Will Happen.

How often do you hear, "I knew that was going to happen."
How did you know?
Did you think it was going to happen?

The words you use affect the way you think.
The way you think affects your life.

If you think success, you will have much more chance of being successful than you will if you think failure.

Imagine if every person who went to compete in the Olympic Games said, "Oh gee, I'm no good, I'm going to fail." Every person who has ever competed in the Olympic Games believed they could win. They had commitment and belief. They set goals with ambition.

They thought positively.

How many times have you heard about competitors trying to psych each other out with mind power?

Every ballerina knows the work and time it took to get up on pointe. Some dancers start at 4 years old, and it is years before they get on pointe, but they have a dream to be on pointe and they work to it.

The body can't distinguish between what is real and what is imagined. So if you are prone to daydream, make sure it is what you want. If you imagine yourself old crippled and ugly, you may find that's what you get. Then you will end up saying, "I knew I'd end up like that." Well if you imagine it, it will be. So picture yourself how and where you want to be.

Picture yourself at the weight you want, in the house you want, in the car you want, in the clothes you want.

Pretend that around you are lots of Angels. They are apprentice Angels. Very enthusiastic, keen to help, but sometimes they don't get things quite right.

If you say, "I am fat, lazy, depressed," they say, "Ok, we'll do it." Beware of these Angels; make sure you say exactly what you want them to hear. So say:

> "My body is fit and healthy.
> Money comes easily to me."

I am successful at all I do.

My body is fit and healthy

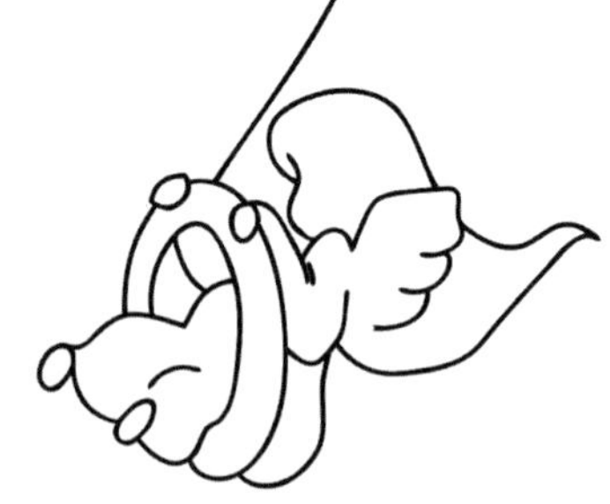

Every time you make a negative statement, stop, tell them you didn't mean that, and replace it with a positive statement. Imagine they are with you always (they will help you find your keys, if you lose them). Be careful what you say, they are listening, and they will even give you what you don't ask for.

It's hard to believe you are thin, when you are not.
However you need to stop saying you are fat!
The mind will hold a picture of fat, and the Angels will think that is what you want. Everything you say, your mind takes on board and the Universe and the Angels are listening, and they reinforce it for you.

Praise yourself for all your good points, and literally ignore the ones you don't like. Think about how old you are. Do you say, "Oh dear I'm 30. 40. 50. 60," as if it is the oldest age in the world? Or do you say I'm ONLY 30. 40. 50. 60?

Hope is something we all have and need. Not the "I hope she wears something decent" or, "I hope she can make a cup of tea." Real hope is the hope that wants every newborn baby to be perfect, the hope that a marriage will last, the hope that your children will grow to be successful, capable adults. The hope, that we will find cures for diseases.

Hope
leads to dreams

Dreams
lead to aspiration

Aspirations
lead to achieving your goals

There is a plaque that says, "Dream, shoot for the moon; even if you miss, you will be among the stars." Some find this a sweet saying, but another interpretation of it could be, head for Sydney, but if you only make it to Dubbo that's ok.

If you want the moon, go get it.

Hope will lead to dreams and dreams will lead to aspiring to what you want. All the hope and all the dreams in the world will not get you anywhere unless you stand up and Do.

Do something, do anything, but do!

If you have a hope, make it a dream, if you have a dream, make it something to aspire to. Own it, take responsibility for it and make it happen. It's the only life you have, so make it a positive one.
Even if the end result is - this is all crazy - it's still nicer to be positive and happy, and enjoy being who you are meant to be, than to be worried, exhausted, and hating yourself and everyone else.

If you are happy, your family will be happy.

Write Your Own Affirmations

1. Affirmations need to be written in the present.By saying "I will" it is in the future. "I will be happy", "I will be successful", "I will be living in abundance." These are all statements in the future, so the Angel will leave it in the future. "I am happy", "I am successful." "I am living in abundance," puts it NOW so your Angel can deal with it now.

Life is wonderful
Life gets better every day
My dreams are reality.

2. Affirmations need to be written in the positive. An affirmation cannot contain a negative. "Don't have an accident", "don't forget" "I will not be late for work," these are all in the negative. "I drive safely," "I remember," and "I arrive on time," are all positive affirmations.

3. Affirmations should lift you up and make you feel good about yourself. Believe in them, remember you are unique, special, and have a right to your place in the Universe.

Affirmations

Take a look at the following affirmations and see if any of them appeal to you. There are many to choose from. Write them down and place them all over the house so you will see them and say them.

On the bathroom mirror,
On the pantry door
On the fridge
Above the taps
On the outside of the shower screen
so you can read through the glass
Above the stove so you can read them as you cook
On the washing machine

Everywhere!!!

If you get strange looks from friends and family, they will change their minds when they see it working for you.

Pick out about 5 or so that you relate to and watch them work.

I am all that I want to be.

I achieve my full potential.

I improve my mind everyday.

My ability to increase my wealth is infinite.

My thoughts are constructive and productive.

I am surrounded with an abundance of opportunity.

There is always abundance in every area of my life.

I am in control of my thoughts.

I am surrounded by abundance.

I am a creator.

I create wealth every day.

I have successful friends.

I am open to new opportunities.

My circumstances improve every day.

My thoughts and habits improve daily.

I make intelligent decisions towards creating wealth.

I associate with successful people.

I have the power to change my life.

I contribute to the lives of others.

I take action to achieve my goals.

Opportunities flow to me.

I give my best thoughts to improving myself.

I am grateful for all the wealth flowing into my life.

The Universe wants me to receive all I want to have.

I give thanks continuously for the good things in my life.

I expect fantastic things to happen to me every day.

I am surrounded by abundance and goodness.

I surround myself with the best life has to offer.

All the money I desire flows into my life.

I complete my goals.

I do all I can in a day.

I am strong and efficient.

I am efficient in my daily tasks.

I make every day a successful day.

I concentrate on the completion of every task.

Each successful action leads to more success.

I concentrate on small details of my work.

I put my best effort into everything I do.

I communicate well with others.

I pursue all opportunities.

I plan for my future

My faith in the Universe is strong.

I use my faith and purpose to complete my tasks.

Mistakes are just a learning tool. I learn from the past.

I consider others in my abundance.

I create the circumstances I desire.

Every action I take is successful.

I express my faith with gratitude.

I meet every challenge.

I make intelligent decisions.

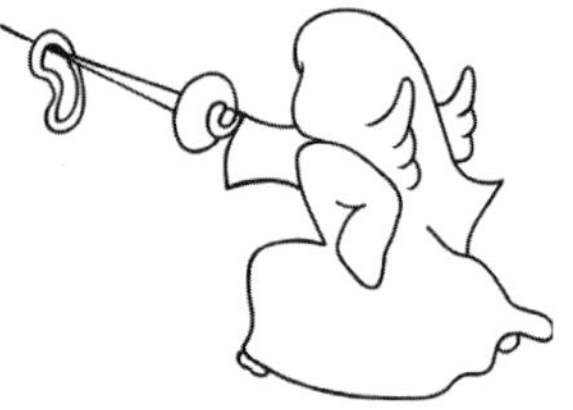

When days are not so great

Blues days are when you have a nasty, awful feeling. No energy or enthusiasm, finding no purpose in your day.

Often it is years later when you look back and you can finally work out why you were so depressed. Of course if there is a tragedy of some sort which led to the blueness you know exactly why.

Don't ask any Angel for you to die. That is not in their power. However, they will hold your hand and be positive for you. Remember, the Angel trying to help you could still be learning, and you need to be direct and clear with her. For those who are not feeling up to coping with life, all this will seem a little silly. It's difficult to be imagining great things when you can't get out of bed.

Start small.... Baby steps.

Set some goals, no matter how silly they seem. Try for 6 goals a day you can start with:

1. Get out of bed
2. Have a shower
3. Brush your teeth
4. Put on deodorant
5. Brush your hair
6. Get dressed.

If you only achieve two of them, well done! Try for three tomorrow. Eventually you can drop the first one and add one more new one, as you will be completing the first one without setting the goal. Try to dress well. You don't have to put on formal wear, but if someone comes to see you, you won't be in your nightwear, or wearing something dowdy. Dress well for you.

When you are done with the first 6 goals move on to others. It may be:

Make the bed
Tidy the bedroom
Have some food
Phone a friend
Go for a walk, go with the friend

Tell yourself how pleased you are with yourself
Work in the garden
Go fishing.

Any small achievement is an achievement.
Be proud you made the effort.

Sometimes being positive feels like the hardest thing in this world to do. If you are really angry, hurt or upset, take time to examine these feelings.

Understand what part you have played in the creation of these feelings.

At no time deny how you feel, that is just delusional.

Work though it and tell yourself, "It's all ok."

Anger can be destructive and help is all around. On occasion it may be necessary to get professional help, but get help before the anger can seriously hurt you or someone else.

Acknowledge your feelings, don't run from them. Examine them and get help if you need to, keep saying positive affirmations.

Distract yourself with positive statements until your focus shifts, even if at the time you can't relate to the statement.

I sleep well and wake refreshed

Sleep

It seems so many people keep saying they can't sleep. If you want sleep, ask for it and try to do things that help to relax you,

Breathing techniques
Meditation
Listen to music
Aromatherapy
Have a routine
Make sure you are comfortable
Try exercise, wear yourself out
Seek help from qualified people.

If you don't believe you will sleep, you won't.
Start to believe that you sleep well and wake refreshed,
You have to affirm your sleep.
If all else fails just chat to the Angels, they will try to give you inspiration, and remember to be clear.

My life is blessed

Gratitude

Thank you is appreciated everywhere. Thank others, and be grateful they are in your life.

Thankfulness and gratitude are important parts of affirmations. Gratitude can change the way you view things and give you a feeling of peace and well being. Try it and see how much it can change the acceptance of things around you. We have all heard the story of the person who cried because they had no shoes, until they saw a man who had no feet (Mahatma Gandhi). We all can give thanks for what we have.

Have a book to write down the good things in your life. At first you may say that there is not a lot of good, but if you can read this, you have eyes and an education. That is more than some people have. In your book write the good things that happened today. If you are stuck, you can start with the fact that you woke up, you had a wash, you have clothes to put on, you have breakfast, and so on. Once you can look at all the good things in your life and be grateful, it puts you in a better state of mind. Appreciate what you have achieved, and you will feel successful. This allows you to be open to the good things life has to offer and to attract more.

Every day try to do something for someone else. A phone call to a lonely person, make a coffee for a friend. It can be a small thing, or a big thing. Even better is to do something loving for someone when they will never know who did it.

Thank the day

Take time to think about all the things you use each day with no regard for them. How would your day be if when you get out of bed and go to the bathroom the toilet is missing? It's not there and there is a hole in the ground to use? There is no hot water in the shower, just one cold tap... This is not a good start to the day! You go to make coffee and all the cups are gone. The day continues, there is no seat in your car, your phone is missing, you have no pen... you get the idea. Imagine how happy you feel when they all come back.

Take time to openly thank all the things in your life that you use and enjoy. Be grateful for the toilet, the shower, the seat in your car, your phone, your pen. Be thankful for waking up in the morning, in a bed with blankets.

The list is endless. You can thank your kitchen, the stove, the food. Bless your pot plants and thank them for the joy they give you. See if it changes your perception of everything in your life.

These small but amazingly special changes in your life can be done in private, no one needs to know, but the Angels will hear.

I find happiness in the small things

Goal Setting

Try two note pads for goal setting, one for your daily goals and one for anything else that you need or want. It's really just a list.

You can have many lists, like a shopping list, just to remind you of certain things. Lists can be anything you want to do, from buying cat food, to collect dry cleaning, to booking a holiday, catching up with friends. Add to your list a few things you keep putting off and work your way through them.

You can have a daily, weekly, monthly, yearly, decade or lifetime list. Not everything on the list has to be done on the day, it can roll over, but eventually you will get them all done. The constant reminder helps keep things in the front of your mind.

Planning and setting goals are part of the organized person's life. The very organized person always has a diary with them to keep their life on track. Buy a diary and consult it daily to remind you what is happening in your life.

"The difference between a dream and a goal,,,
A goal has a date put on it." Dr Phil

Choice or Chance

Is your path to your destiny choice or chance?

So much of your life is made up of the choices made by you. Every choice you have made has brought you to this very moment in your life. You are responsible for your choices, no one else.

Do you always run late?
That is your choice.

Do you want to be on time?
That is your choice.

Do you say that there are not enough hours in the day, that you have no time, that you need to make time?
You cannot make time; you can be in control of it.
How much time do you need?
Are you taking on too much?
Do you need to say no?
Do you need to plan your time better?

Being punctual is a choice. No one likes to wait for you while you are late. No one wants to hear your excuses. Start by making the decision to be on time. Plan what time you need to be ready, and if that means the bed is left unmade, so be it. Next time you can make the bed and be on time.

Plan to be ready on time for one week. Set your alarm clock 30 minutes earlier than usual, and get organized. If you say that you don't want to get up that early then you have made your choice.

Of course there are times when the car doesn't start, or there is an unexpected event that will detain you, but you need to make a commitment to being able to do things in a set time.

I Choose

When you feel you can't afford something, and you say, "I can't afford that" then that is the message you send to the Universe. Try saying, "I can afford this, I will get it later," or simply, "I will get it." Choose to have it, or choose to buy it at a time when you can afford it. Instead of saying, "I must vacuum the floor, I have to make the bed" try, "I choose to do this." choosing to do it could lighten your feelings from "I must" and "I have to."

Meet Kelly...

A lovely lady with three children, two attend school and one is a baby. She hates mornings, She tells everyone they are a nightmare. Remember Angels are listening and will help Kelly get her nightmare. Her daughter can't find a shoe; she has lost her drink bottle. The morning gets worse, until finally they get into the car and go to school. The traffic is bedlam and they are usually late. Kelly goes home feeling defeated and a failure. The house is a mess, the bathroom and bedroom need work, the kitchen is the usual mess of breakfast remnants. Things could be easier, but Kelly just can't commit to being organized. She could help the children find their school uniforms, shoes and drink bottles the night before.

If she was up 30 minutes earlier, she would be dressed and have her room tidy before having to attend to the children. Spending a few minutes in each bedroom with each child, she could teach the children to make the beds and tidy the room.

If she wanted to, she could leave home earlier. She wouldn't be in the traffic and could park closer to the school entry. If it was too early to send the children in, she could read to them or talk to them about their day.

Of course she doesn't have to do any of these things, she can continue going the way she is, but if she thinks it's a nightmare it will be. To start turning it into a dream morning, she has to take responsibility for her choices.

You are born, and you will die. What is the bit in the middle going to be like? Do you believe in destiny, that no matter what you do, you will end up where you are meant to be? Think of the bit in the middle as a very wide road. It leads to the end of your life. However, it is up to you which part of this wide road you walk. One side is smooth, easy, and warm, you can see the beauty around you and enjoy the walk. The other side is filled with potholes and puddles. The road is so bumpy that it is difficult to take your eyes off the road for fear you will stumble. It is the same road, and the destination may be the same but what sort of journey will you choose to have? Will you choose to walk on the side that is filled with the contentment to love and be loved? To be non judgmental, and accepting of others? To be open and willing to count your blessings? To be able to wake every day and say I am blessed and believe it?

These are *your* choices.

Do you find yourself being critical of others? This can be infectious. One person starts to be critical and then the next person starts, and it feeds off itself. If you are being critical of others, start to think about things you really like and are accepting of. It is a habit that can be broken.

Your choice.

On this road of life, at times you may find you have wandered over the harder side of life. The road is steep and rough. Choose to see the good around you, call on your Angels to help. Stay positive and loving. Help others when you can. Stay in touch with the friends you want to walk this path with. Ignore the one that you wish to move on from and they will move to another path. You have your life in your hands by simply choosing to change.

"If it is meant to be...it is up to me"
Make things happen.

You are playing Solitaire on the computer and you find yourself stuck on a game that you can't solve, so you hit restart. The same cards appear in the same order and you keep putting down the same cards and you get the same result, do you really imagine you are going to get a different result? This can happen in your life. Every day you hit the restart button and wonder why nothing changes. Sometimes you need to start a new game, or at least play the game differently.

Your choice.

You want to lose weight, but you skip breakfast and eat biscuits and chocolate.

Your choice.

Decide, you either want to eat whatever you want, and love yourself for it, or you want to lose weight and love yourself for it.

Your choice.

Meet Michelle...

She found a photo of herself when she was a teenager and put it on the fridge with a message to the Universe that she wanted to look as she did in the photo. It's a good thing to have a photo of yourself to remind you of what it is you want and ask the Universe to assist you in your effort. She explained this to her friend. To test Michelle's understanding of commitment the friend asked her to name an Olympian. She named a well known swimmer. Her friend suggested that although the swimmer may have put a photo of an Olympian on his fridge, he still had to get in the pool and swim the laps. He was up at all strange hours to go and train. He didn't sit on the couch watching swimmers going up and down a pool and expecting the Universe to do the rest. So put the photo on the fridge, aspire to be as you want to be, but it will mean getting out on the footpath, and not buying the biscuits. You will still need to put in the hard yards. Believe you will succeed, get your brain conditioned to the fact that you will achieve the desired results.

Your choice.

The Universe will assist when you make your choices. It can often put the ideas into your head and lead you to find the photo to put on the fridge. Do you want to believe that it will happen if it is meant to? That works sometimes, but if you really want to live your life to the fullest degree, be prepared to take responsibility for it. Sometimes your choice is to take a chance. Sometimes your choice may be to leave it to chance, either way, that choice was made by you.

Free Will

All humans have free will, Angels can only guide and support, they cannot make you do anything.

Quite often your choices have a direct affect on the offerings the Angels bring.

They can be seen whispering in your ear to try to get the right result. They weep when the wrong decision is made.

You know when decisions are not the right ones. If you are ever in doubt, ask the Angels for guidance, they will be your conscience,

However, you can never use the excuse the Angels made me do it. They do not have the power, and even if they did, they would not use the power to override your free will.

Free will is yours, a gift from the Universe.

I meet every challenge

Be Careful What You Wish For

Often the question is asked, and the request is made, but are you ready for the answer? Many people don't think it through. You may ask for something but if you are not ready, you will waste it. Do you truly feel worthy to be supplied? Here is a well known story. (author unknown)

A man is in a small fishing boat when the weather changes and he is in serious trouble. He prays to God to save him, and along comes a fishing trawler and offers him help. He refuses the help saying God will save him. He prays again. Presently a cargo ship offers to take him, and the man refuses again with the same reply. Finally a huge ocean liner comes to his aid and the man is still adamant that he is ok because God is going to save him. The man dies.

He goes to heaven and asks God why he has been forgotten and his prayer not answered. God explained that he had sent a fishing trawler, a cargo ship and a liner and the man refused the help each time.

A woman living on her own was having difficultly maintaining her garden, so she asked her Angels to help. A retired elderly man offers to help, as he was happy to work in the garden. He looked at the garden and made some interesting suggestions about what could be done. She didn't like his suggestions, so instead of saying what she wanted, she told him not to bother that she would manage.

Many times help is sent just to be refused. First consider if you want to hand it over to the Universe or are you looking for help on your terms. It's fine to have conditions on the help you require, but try to be open to the help being offered, it may lead to things improving your life.

Do you really want others helping you, or are you looking for guidance to complete something? Are you looking for strength or patience? Be clear with what you want. If you really want help, then hand it over and accept the help that is around you.

If your health is not good you may request to find a healer that will be able to help you solve the problem. Are you willing to follow the advice, maybe stop smoking, do exercise, or change your diet? It is hard to get the result you want when you are asking for help but sending stop signs.

Do you have a business that you would like to be incredibly successful but are scared of the success? If you are successful you will need to employ people, find bigger premises, have the money to pay wages and increase your stock. Your life will change. Is this really what you want? If your requests are not being met, ask yourself are you ready to receive? Look at the ways you may be sabotaging yourself.

When your request is slow in coming, ask for the help of patience, and know that when the time is right, you will get the help, as long as you are open to the many forms in which it comes. It may come in a form that you dislike and you may have to check your prejudices, for on occasion, you may have to learn something before you get the help.

Don't give up.

There may be many reasons that you are not ready to receive but don't give up. Ask to be shown the reasons, work through them but never give up. The moment you say, "This isn't working," or "I give up," you stop the help. Give your request to the Universe, your subconscious, the Angels, God, or whatever will bring you the peace to keep working, keep trying, and keep believing. How many times have you heard someone say, "I have always wanted one of those" or "I asked for that years ago."

It will all happen in its time.
Be ready when it does.

Imagining The Now

Make a positive statement; do you really believe it will happen?

When you sit in an aeroplane, you have no idea how it takes off and travels through the sky, but it does.

You buy a ticket to travel on an old steam engine. You arrive at the station, but nothing is happening. You feel that you have your ticket and the train should be ready. So you stand on the station feeling cross that it's not going.

However coal is being loaded on, eventually the fire will be lit, the coal shoveled in and the heat will rise. This needs to be attended to carefully, stoking the fire, watching the water doesn't run out, getting the steam to the right pressure. When all is ready, and not before, the train starts to move. Very slowly at first, so slowly you can walk beside it. It gains speed, and you walk faster, you are slightly out of breath, it keeps gaining, and you have to run to keep up. It pulls away and you are left behind. Instead of getting on board and believing the train will move, you were busy wanting to know how the train would move and why it took so long. Go about your life believing in what you want to happen. It is happening now, just not in a way that you can see, hear or touch it.

There is a play you have wanted to see for a long time. You are excited and you go to the theatre 10 months early. You sit in the seat with great expectation and find there is nothing going on. The stage is empty and you feel despondent and grumpy. You thought this was happening now. You wanted to see it now. You leave disappointed and refuse to return later to see the play.

The day you sat in the auditorium there was so much going on. So many people were working hard.

- Production meetings were happening.
- Lighting directors were plotting the lighting.
- Costume designers were in discussion with the costume makers.
- Sound engineers were working with stage managers.
- Sets were being designed and discussed with set builder and scenic artists.
- Actors were being auditioned and rehearsals were starting.
- Contracts were being drawn up for the artist and front of house merchandise.

The work happening before the event was immense, but it was all going on behind the scenes and couldn't be seen. Finally the play opens and it's wonderful. So many professional people are involved in putting on the play or moving the train.

The same applies to the Universe when you put in a request. You may want a car, a job, a partner, a house, a holiday. Try to imagine how you will feel when this desire happens. Tell yourself it is happening now! I have my dream house/ job/ partner/ car. It is all working behind the scenes. Cogs are slowly moving for you to work to your heart's desire. It may not be in your reality, but believe that the Universe is doing it.

Think of Angels listening to your every word and, like all the workers bringing the play together, they are finding ways to put on this production. Then suddenly you say it's not going to happen. The Angels stop working. They are listening to your every word. So when you get back on track and say it will work, they start to work again.

Angels are working so hard to get you where you want to be. It could be that you need to get other jobs in order to meet the right people, or learn the right skills before you get the dream position.

The same might apply to your dream house. Even a visit to the doctor may be where you meet your partner. Who knows? This is why sending positive requests in the present are important. It is being worked on, you just can't see it.

Have faith, keep believing.

The Angels are listening and waiting to hear any changes. Make sure you say exactly what you want them to hear. How often do you hear some one say:

If that hadn't happened I would never had met...
If I hadn't gone there I would never have seen...

The Angels can deliver the negative as well as the positive.

I am creative and inspired

Meet Lyn

Lyn had a reasonable understanding of the way of the Universe, however she found life tough, and had a tendency to live in the negative. If you asked her how her day was, her usual rely was, "Oh you know, same crap, different bucket." It was pointed out to her by various friends that she was inviting crap to be put in her bucket, but she would laugh and say, "I know."

Finally the crap came, in the form of breast cancer. She withdrew contact from everyone and decided to tackle it with all she knew how. After treatment, she no longer had breast cancer, or the crap attitude. The cancer made her realize how precious her life and everything in it is. No longer came the reply, "same crap different bucket," now her outlook is more accepting, as she sees her world as a wonderful place with loving and supportive friends.

Now when she has a tiny doubt about her health she says, "My body is fit and healthy, I maintain good health." Her comment is that even if at that time she doesn't believe it, she keeps repeating it until she gets distracted to do something else. She just won't allow any space in her life for the negative.

I resolve all issues in my favour

Karma

Some believe that karma comes through from previous lives, but to keep it simple this is about present day karma.

Are you always the best you can possibly be?
Do you work to the best of your ability?
Are you honest with yourself, and others?

The smallest things taken without consent will all add up. Karma is just for you. It is an integral part of your journey through your life. No one else has to answer to it. All the good, and the not so good, will be recorded. You will be the judge at the end. You will see how every decision you have made that affected another person had a consequence. It is important to be aware of using things that are not yours to use.

Picture this...

You are at work, and you need a stamp to post a personal letter. You know that a colleague has stamps in her drawer, so you help yourself to a stamp with the attitude that she won't mind. Later in the kitchen, you see a container with biscuits in it. You help yourself to two of them saying to yourself that no one will miss them.

That evening you are at the gym, and you sign in with a beautiful pen. You like the flow, weight and style of the pen. You take the pen and put it in your bag with the theory that you pay enough in gym fees, so you deserve it and the gym can afford it. You think that in the great scheme of things a stamp a biscuit and a pen is no big deal, it happens all the time everybody does it, people take things without permission. If you take something that is not yours you are sending a message that it is ok to take things from others.

Let's look at this from an Angel's point of view. Remember they have simple ways of looking at things.

You take the stamp with the feeling that it is justified because you think the owner of the stamp didn't mind. What if they did mind, what if they had the stamps for a purpose? Do you know how taking the stamp affected them? By saying the person didn't mind, you are telling the Universe that as long as a person thinks you don't mind, it's ok for them to take your things.

So an Angel can say it's ok for someone to take your stuff because you took someone else's property with the justification that they didn't mind.

The same applies to the biscuits. You took them, saying they will never be missed, so if someone feels that your diamond earrings/

cufflinks will never be missed, do they have the right to take them?

Angels and the Universe will feel that if the justification is for the biscuits, it should apply to the earrings. It's irrelevant if you will miss them or not. You took the biscuits with the belief that they wouldn't be missed. but you will never know. The same applies with the earrings, you may miss them but they were taken by someone who thought you wouldn't.

What about the pen? You really liked the pen, so you found justification in the fact that the gym was a prosperous business and you felt your fees entitled you to take it. If someone earns less than you, and feels that you can afford to buy another, is it ok for them to take it from you?

If someone wants something of yours and they feel justified in taking it, the Universe will say ok because you did it. It sets up a chain reaction.

You steal something, so someone steals from you and they steal from them, so on it goes.

You decide if you take something without permission, then you have no reason to complain if something is taken from you without permission.

Our Angels also remember the way you treat people. If you treat others with little respect, care and love, you are sending a message that it's acceptable to be treated in that manner.

Be aware of your treatment of others, and if you put something in your pocket that belongs to someone else, it will be remembered and karma may return to you many years later when you least expect it.

Constant complaining will have people complain to you.
Being critical will bring criticism.
Remember that what you give out will come back to you.

However if someone has wronged you and they have bad luck, those who believe that karma is working on your behalf could be disappointed. Being happy in watching others suffering is revenge not karma. Just be aware that in time they will be judged on their actions just as you will be judged on yours.

Seeing the positive

Losing your job can be devastating.

Did you really like your job, or did you complain about it?

You can't complain about losing a job you didn't want, or never liked. If the Angels heard you complaining, they probably thought you didn't want it anyway and helped you to be free of it.

If you loved your job, it is hard to accept termination, but be grateful for the time you had it, doing something you loved. Is there now something better for you? Of course there is.

Think about the fact that the job served a purpose and be grateful for it. Make a list of all the things you learnt in the time you were there. The people you met and helped. What did you do for the first time?

If it is your first job, you now have a work history, and new skills to use. Imagine you are in the perfect place for you. Do you need to do some training to get the perfect position?

I have faith in the Universe

Imagination

Imagination is one of your greatest gifts, it fuels artists, inventors, songwriters, musicians, writers, teachers and many more. Scientists imagine the outcomes before attempting to prove them scientifically.

You alone limit your imagination. Nothing is started without someone imagining it first. Think of the imaginings at the Apple Corporation. Not all things imagined will work, but they can lead to something that will.

Creative people use their imagination to make their creations.

John Lennon wrote a song about it. Put your imagination to great use, put all your ideas on paper, write them down.

Imagine doing something you always wanted to do. Enjoy the experience, do it often.

Imagine yourself in a peaceful place, totally relaxed, and drift into this imaginary place.

Imagine Angels surrounding you waiting to be called upon to help.

The Unexpected

Sometimes things happen and we can't understand why. We feel so helpless that we want to blame the Universe, God, Angels and anything else that will help to get through the pain.

You don't have to do anything to deserve bad luck. God doesn't punish you by making things go wrong for you. He doesn't make disease, war, accidents, or anything nasty. The Universe doesn't have it in for you.

Meet Jacqui...

Jacqui owned a dog who was the most beautiful dog in Jacqui's world. The dog was named Miss Molly. Miss Molly was a big black standard poodle. She was one of the family and Jacqui was devoted to her.

Miss Molly became sick and at 6 years old, after a long battle with her health, she died. Jacqui was completely bereft with the passing of Miss Molly and was heard to comment about how cruel the Universe was.

The Universe didn't make Miss Molly sick or take her away, it just happened. Jacqui soon came to realise this and so, rather than blaming the Universe for the passing of her precious Miss Molly, she rejoiced in the fact that she had been blessed with Miss Molly for 6 years. She realised that Miss Molly had been there to share in her life, and in return she had always been there for Miss Molly.

Now, a new poodle has entered Jacqui's life and she is starting to train and love a new member of the family, but with the knowledge that Miss Molly is always with her.

Things just happen. In human form there is so much to learn and experience. This is the path and journey you have undertaken.

The Universe will help you through the tough times, have faith in yourself and the Universe to deliver you to where you are meant to be.

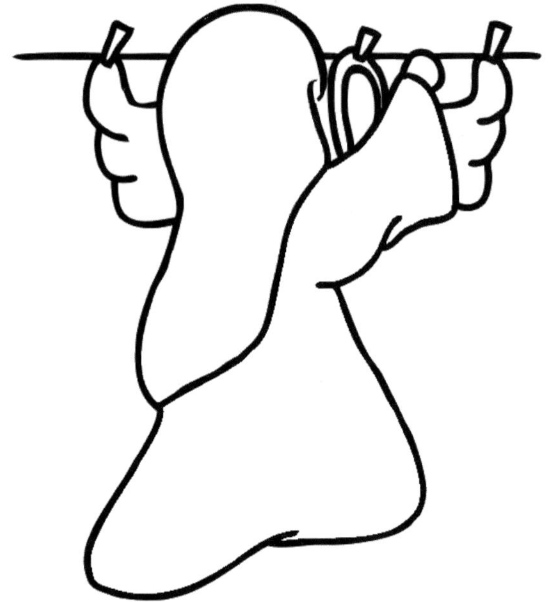

I can, and I do succeed

Universal Understanding

Some of you will come to understand universal understanding while you are young, some will have to wait until they are in their later life to be enlightened. There is no reason for this, it's just when the time is right for you. If someone tried to tell you about the Universal Consciousness while you were a baby, you would have little chance of understanding. When you have completed some of the things you need to know, the time will be right.

Some people go to school, get a job, and may stay at that position until they retire. They marry, buy a house, have children and stay in that house all their life. They never question if there is any more to life and they are content with what life has given them. Then there are others who ask the question.

If you ask the question, the Universe will start to give you answers. You can never go back to the way you were. Sometimes you will wish that you never started on the universal knowledge path, but you can't go back. Once you take on the fact that you are the one responsible for everything in your life, things will be different for you.

Facing Facts and Acceptance

It's all very well to think positively and have great affirmations; it's great to have inspiration and motivation, but at times you may have to be realistic. Although, like magic, things can happen in your life all the time. You make decisions and take responsibility for yourself.

If you are 60 years old and you suddenly decide you want to be a prima ballerina, you may have made it a bit tough for the Angels to follow through on that one, but you can take dancing lessons, learn the tango, or tap dance. You will still be able to dance, even take ballet lessons. The same applies to singing, if you have always wanted to sing, join a choir.

There may be a 60 year old somewhere trying to be a prima ballerina, and they can be given all the love and support in the world and maybe they will make it. Who would know?

Don't give your energy to things you can't change. If someone or a situation is causing you problems, and there is nothing you can do about it, just send them good and loving thoughts.

Avoid all conflict with them.

Some things in life you feel you will never change, so accept them.

If you really don't like brussel sprouts, or beetroot or some other food, there is no point in telling yourself that you love them.

To be spending your time saying you love beetroot when you don't is just pointless. The fact is that some people love them, and can eat them everyday, you on the other hand can choose to enjoy other foods. You don't spend energy on trying to change the brussel sprout.

The same thinking is applied to people, places and situations.

If you don't like someone or something pretend they are a brussel sprout (or something else if you like sprouts)

Accept that they have a place and a reason for being and that they give joy to some people, just not to you. Having imaginary conversations with them or thinking too much about them is just stealing your energy, You may lose sleep over it, but the brussel sprout will be sleeping like a baby.

It is far healthier to be thinking about the ones you love, and who love you, that worrying about the ones who don't.

I reach my true potential

Inspiration

Is there someone who gives you inspiration? Is there someone you admire? It doesn't matter who they are. It can be a cartoon character or a role in a movie.

Maybe someone has overcome incredible odds and has moved you.

Mother Teresa, Leigh Anne Tuohy, Nelson Mandela, Marie Curie, there are many many more. Find photos of them to help you keep the flame of inspiration alive in you.

If their image can help you to aspire to the best you can be then use it. Whatever it takes. Use them as tools to create the life you want.

The image of a little Angel may play a part. She will be there to listen and help, but be careful how you ask and be ready for the answer.

Affirmations	Goal setting
Decisions	Karma
Choice	Being positive
Gratitude	Acceptance

All these things will help you to live the life you are meant to have.

Trust in the life that you have taken on. You are here to learn and grow. Sometimes it grows in ways that you never thought of and will surprise you.

Stay positive.
The only thing that will stop you
is the reason you give yourself for not succeeding.

Time To Congratulate You

You have all heard the question, "Is the glass half full, or is the glass half empty?" If you say the glass is half full, it's said you are an optimist, If you say the glass is half empty, you are considered a pessimist. In reality, the glass is neither full nor empty; it is just half a glass of water.

A bottle of beer sits on the table. An alcoholic walks by and considers it to be poison. He thinks of it as the catalyst to all his problems. Another man has been working in the garden all day and walks inside to see a cold bottle of beer on the table and celebrates it as the nectar of the Gods. He sits and drinks the beer with relish and reflects on his work.

The bottle is neither poison nor nectar, it is simply a bottle of beer. It has no idea what anyone thinks of it.

You decide if it's good or bad. It's all in the mind of the person seeing the beer.

The concept of good and bad is subjective.

Something that is good for some can be devastating for others.

Everyone is different, with different needs and different wants. If you have a different view on things, that doesn't make it wrong. What is your view of yourself?

Are you more critical of yourself than others?

Many people are hard on themselves. Seeking perfection in all they do. Seeking approval from others.

The best approval is self-approval, to approve of yourself and others. How often do you say to yourself, "Well done, good job, fantastic work?"

When did you last look in the mirror and say, "You look great?" Have you ever complemented yourself on a great meal?

It's time to congratulate YOU.

The bed is made! Good job.
The washing's done! Fantastic work.
Shopping done and put away! Well done.

Try it for one day, everything you do congratulate yourself on each achievement.

Thank Yourself

Many books will tell you to love yourself. This is a difficult concept for many people. Much of your conditioning is from childhood and makes this a hard thing to do.

You can start with treating yourself as you would treat others.

When you can congratulate yourself for the great job you have done then say thank you to yourself as well.

If your friend/child does something for you, you tell them what a great job they have done or how wonderful it was, and then you thank them. Now do it for you.

Make the bed... good job, thank you.

Treat yourself as well as you treat the ones you love and care for. If you look in the mirror and your first thought is "I look like crap," ask yourself, would you say that to someone you love. If your friend made that statement, you would reassure them. If your child said it, you would tell them how beautiful and special they are. Yet you say these things to yourself.

You are a unique, individual, dynamic child of the Universe, and the Universe and Angels love you.

Start to say nice things to yourself. Get a group of friends to help. Make a pact with your friends to stop the self-criticism. Find friends who will allow you to only say loving words to yourself.

This is so important. You have value, and you need to recognize your true value.

Affirmation Angels are listening to all your words, every word that leaves your mouth. Being critical to you is not helpful to them. They don't understand you being critical of your body, so if you say your life is full of crap, they will deliver the crap.

Don't wait for the approval of others, tell yourself "great work" when you complete a task. Thank yourself for doing such a good job. Imagine a chorus of Angels clapping in glorious applause.

Take a bow they'll love it.
Just try it.

Don't feel silly no one is watching except the Angels and they will be ecstatic that you are being good to you. Try it, see if it lifts your spirits, and makes you feel better about your day.

Ask yourself, "What can I do to make this day better for me?"

At first you may not think of anything.

You can say an affirmation that your day will be smooth and joyous. It could be to say, "Gee, I'm great!"

After completing every task, say thank you.

Keep saying, "This is a good day, everything I do makes it better."

Sit and think about you and what you really want to do today.

Improve each day and you improve your life.

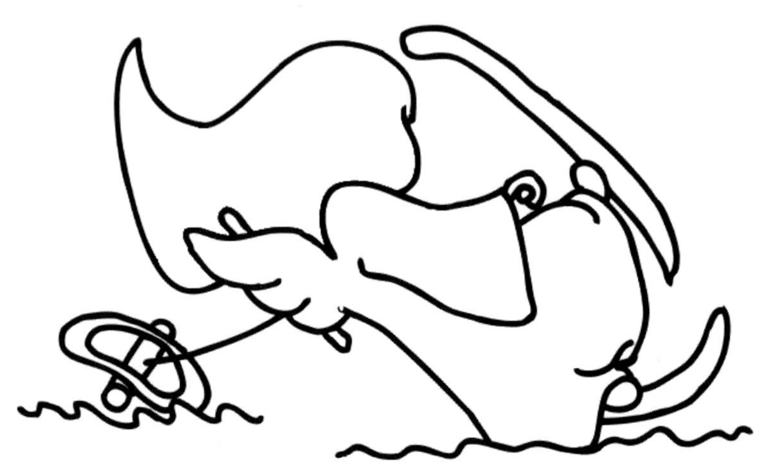

I am free to change my situation

Change is Easy… maybe

Affirmations will help to train your mind to be positive and start to encourage a new state of mind. However change can prove difficult for many. How many times do you start a diet and a friend buys you chocolates? You want to save money and the invitations start to pour through the door.

Change isn't easy for some.

You will think you are sabotaging yourself, you may feel that everyone is sabotaging you.

Imagine for a moment or two:

A child goes to their mother and says that they want to be a ballet dancer. The mother thinks about this and wonders if this is the right choice. She asks the child if they know how much hard work, pain and commitment this will take. She then sets simple tasks and obstacles in the child's life to test if the child is serious about this decision. The mother is not being nasty to her child, she wants to know if this decision is a practical path for her child to take. Now imagine you are the child and the mother the Angel. The Angels want to see how committed you are to the decisions you make and what you ask for.

Once you have resolved to commit yourself to what it is you want, you will find that the Universe will work with you.

No one likes change. Staying with what we know is comfortable and everyone likes comfort. To change anything means applying yourself to the task that needs changing. To play an instrument takes years of practice, it's a learning process. Change is similar, it is a process of learning something new, day by day, and forgetting the off notes and enjoying the good notes. Eventually the single notes become a phrase, the phrase becomes a tune, and finally you can play a favourite piece of music.

So next time someone brings you chocolate and you are on a diet, be thankful for the wonderful gift, and share them with everyone at work so you all have one and you are not tempted to eat them all. Your colleagues will enjoy the sharing. If you are running late and you are trying to be on time, just take a deep breath and commit to being on time for the rest of the day. Stay calm, it's just a testing time. Imagine you are on time. Getting worked up won't get you there any more quickly.

If you are serious about saving your money set yourself a budget. This is not easy, but if you want the funds, you will find a way. You can find ways to gift your friends without spending a fortune. Give a voucher for the bearer to be entitled to 4 hours work done by you, or a picnic, an afternoon tea, a back rub, a foot massage, dog walking, lawn mowing, window cleaning, ironing. Be creative and see what you can offer instead of an expensive gift.

Just keep the faith, set your goals, and show the Angels that you are serious about changing.

Some days you will be challenged. Work your way through it. If you slip up one day, you can try again the next.

Don't beat yourself up, just start again with the affirmations. If you are giving up smoking and keep lapsing, don't worry, but keep trying. Don't give up, giving up. Even if it takes years to give up the cigarettes, it will be worth it in the end.

Some thrive on the challenge so be careful of comparing yourself to others. They have a different path to you, and they may find other steps in life more challenging than you. Everyone has their own story, their own challenges. Concentrate on your own desires, goals and challenges.

Be sensible about taking on to many challenges at a time.
Take one step at a time.

I face my fears
and reach my dreams

Do Not Compare

Don't compare yourself to others. If the Universe wanted everyone to be the same, there would be a clone factory. You are not the same as anyone else even if you have a twin.

You are individual, different, unique, be proud of that fact. There will always be people you perceive to be better, brighter, more confident, wealthier, happier, thinner, fatter, taller, shorter, the list is endless.

You are responsible for your life.
Just you.

Not someone smarter, better, brighter.
Come to understand how you are perfect.
Some find this hard to believe, and find it complicated. Your life to this date is exactly as it should be, you are learning every day. Start to acknowledge that you are where you should be and the universal plan is perfect.

You are in the perfect place at the perfect time. You are precisely how you are meant to be at this point in your life. If you don't like it, do something to improve it.

Everything you have ever done and experienced has brought you to this point. All is good, all is well. This is the perfect place to access the perfect you. Can things be better? Do you need a plan to improve?

Your Definition Of Success

Success and achievement are not confined to the business world, movie stars, sports and IT people. A successful person is not the one who dies with the biggest bank account.

Define your idea of success.

Is it to climb the corporate ladder? Is it to have a wonderful home with lots of children, or both? You may know someone with 19 grandchildren and see that as a level of success. Someone who has great family ties. The single mother with 6 children who educates them all, is a success story in itself. Children who have survived alcoholic parents are success stories. People who lived though earthquakes and hurricanes can count themselves as successful.

You can have success on your own, with a partner, in a small or large family. What is your idea of success for you? There is no right or wrong answer. Some wealth-driven people go to their grave un-fulfilled, feeling a failure. Some homeless people go to meet their maker with contentment, peace, and a sense of achievement.

You make your destiny each step of the way, and improvement is yours for the asking.

I take responsibility for my actions

The Best You Can Be

Are you being the best you can possibly be? Are you doing the best job you can possibly do? To get the best you need to give your best. Ask yourself, "Is this the best I can do?" If the answer is yes, good work, If the answer is no, try again until you are satisfied it is the best it's going to be.

Have visions and dreams.

Set goals and achievements.

Put plans into actions.

Take responsibility for yourself and your mistakes.

Learn from mistakes and move on.

Remember to say thank you for all you have and all you can be.

Be the best you can be. You deserve it.

Getting a Plan

Has anyone ever said to you, "I believe you can."
Have they said. "I believe in you."
If not, what are you waiting for, say it now.

Don't listen to people who are unsupportive. They often can't comprehend what you are wanting to achieve and rather than see you disappointed, they will try to talk you out of the things you want to try to achieve. Many old school people don't want to encourage you, just in case you fail and they will feel responsible. Just understand they are worried for you and they are trying to protect you in their own way. If they can't say, "I believe you can," you say it to you.

You need to stay focused on your outcome, holding your dream. Mix with like minded people, who can understand your efforts.

Ask yourself these questions

What do I want out of life?
What is it I really want to do?
Where would I like to be in 2-5 years time?
What would I like to be doing in 2, 5, 10 years time?

For the corporate person the answer may be easy. For the athlete preparing for the Olympics the answer will be in the snap of the fingers. Most of the population are not corporate or elite athletes and if you are one of those people who ask these questions and have no clue of an answer, don't despair, you are not alone. Many have lost direction of what they want and the very first thing to know is... that it's ok not to know.

It's time to make a plan.
Small things to start.

A list for one day, and then for two. Set a plan for a week, a month, a year. Before you know it, you will have a five year plan. Buy a corkboard, scrapbook or magnetic board. Cut out pictures, photos, brochures, anything visual to apply to the boards.

Plan 12 months ahead. Maybe book a massage for the first day the children start the new school year. Save up all year if you must, but start something for a yearly event.

Most people spend all year planning their two week holiday.

Try spending two weeks planning your year.

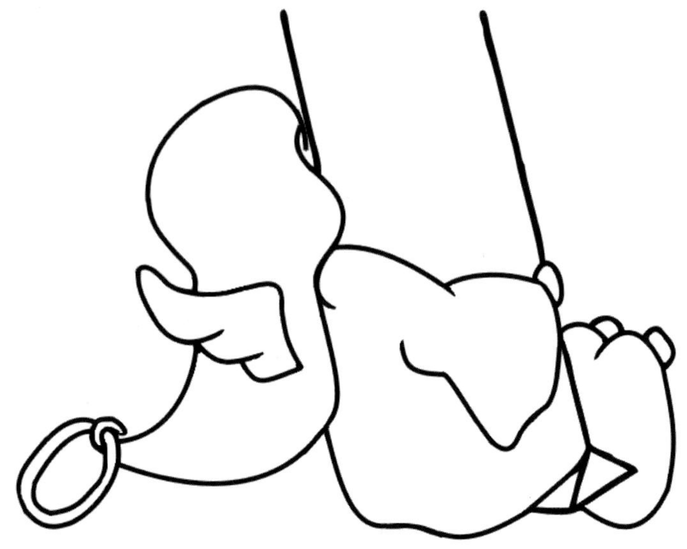

I rejuvenate emotionally spiritually and physically

Self Help Books

These words are not unique. They have all been said before many times by many people. There are hundreds of books on the subject. Read as many as you can, they all have something to offer. If you feel they apply to the corporate world and not to you read them anyway, and then get more books.

Some self help books are written for corporate people wanting wealth and promotion in a big company, others will apply to the person at home, with or without children, the homeless or a wealthy bored housewife. If finances are tight, go to the library, or a second-hand bookstore, buy a book and trade the book in when you have finished it. Find friends and all buy different books and swap them.

Find the one that you resonate with, one will ring true for you. Some are quite confronting, and some may seem frivolous, but they will all be part of your guidance and growth until you decide what is most inspirational and meaningful.

Do not let your circumstances stand in the way of improvement.

Believe you will improve your life.

Therapy

Therapy comes in many forms, and everyone will need some therapy at some time. Going fishing can be very therapeutic. Having lunch with friends can be therapy. Therapy is not necessarily with a trained person, it can be allowing yourself to have some time to yourself, or chatting over problems with a friend. There are hundreds of trained people who offer all kinds of therapy from massage to in-depth psychotherapy.

Take time to nurture yourself, as it will be easier to nurture others if you are nurtured first. A massage once a month, a visit to a kinesiologist or reflexologist, can work wonders for keeping you tuned up. Allow yourself some pampering now and again. There are hundreds of different therapies out there, so find the one that is special for you. Try myotherapy, and if it's not for you try something else. If you can't bear to have your feet touched reflexology is not for you. Look after you first, so you are able to give to others.

If you feel you need more, then a visit to your doctor will find you the counseling you may need, stay positive that you will find the right help and be healed.

Summary

Remember the power of your words. The Angels are listening and want to help at all times, so check every thing you say.

Use affirmations to help train yourself to be positive, and help the Angels know what you want.

Put your words into action, take control of your life.

Define your success and plan to get there. Be the best you can be.

Get help if you need to, help is everywhere.

Love and nurture yourself, be kind to you and remember at all times you are a valued part of the community of mankind.

You are here for a reason, you have purpose.

This is your journey and you will decide how it goes.

You are a worthwhile person and the Universe loves you.

YOU ARE LOVED

Suggested reading.

The Winner's Bible by Dr Kerry Spackman
Any books by Louise Hay.
Any books by Cheryl Richardson.
All books by Andrew Matthews.

The Power Of Your Words

Affirmation Angel

ISBN 9781922175410   Qty

RRP   AU$19.99   .....

Postage within Australia   AU$5.00   .....

TOTAL* $_________

* All prices include GST

Name:..

Address: ....

....

Phone:..

Email: ....

Payment: ❏ Money Order ❏ Cheque ❏ MasterCard ❏ Visa

Cardholders Name:..

Credit Card Number: ....

Signature:...

Expiry Date: ....

Allow 7 days for delivery.

Payment to: Marzocco Consultancy (ABN 14 067 257 390)
PO Box 12544
A'Beckett Street, Melbourne, 8006
Victoria, Australia
admin@brolgapublishing.com.au

BE PUBLISHED

Publish through a successful publisher.
Brolga Publishing is represented through:
- **National** book trade distribution, including sales,
marketing & distribution through **Macmillan Australia.**
- **International** book trade distribution to
    - The United Kingdom
    - North America
    - Sales representation in South East Asia
- **Worldwide e-Book distribution**

For details and inquiries, contact:
Brolga Publishing Pty Ltd
PO Box 12544
A'Beckett St VIC 8006

Phone: 0414 608 494
markzocchi@brolgapublishing.com.au
ABN: 46 063 962 443
(Email for a catalogue request)